I BELIEVE

Trevor Huddleston was born in Bedford in 1913, and was educated at Lancing and Christ Church, Oxford.

After a period in Ceylon and India he was ordained in 1937, and in 1943 went to South Africa as Priest-in-Charge of the Community of the Resurrection's Mission in Sophiatown, and stayed in that country until 1956. He has been a champion of the black people there ever since.

In 1958 Trevor Huddleston became Prior of the London House of the Community of the Resurrection; in 1960 Bishop of Masasi, and in 1968 Bishop of Stepney. He then became Bishop of Mauritius and Archbishop of the Province of the Indian Ocean in 1978. He returned to England in 1983 where he continues to be active in the struggle against apartheid.

I BELIEVE

Reflections on the Apostles' Creed

Trevor Huddleston C.R.

Collins
FOUNT PAPERBACKS

First published in Great Britain by
Fount Paperbacks, London, 1986

Made and printed in Great Britain by
William Collins Sons & Co. Ltd, Glasgow

Dedication

For Pauline Webb
who initiated this most demanding
project and without whose persistent
encouragement it would certainly
not have been completed.

Contents

Preface

This small book was not originally written to be read but to be spoken. I was invited by the World Service of the BBC to give twenty-six four-minute talks on the Apostles' Creed, and these were broadcast over a period of six months. I had to bear in mind that an audience of some twenty-five million people would be hearing what I had to say, that probably the majority of them would not be familiar with the Creed at all, and perhaps that even more would not be Christians.

To say anything in four minutes about the great dogmas of the Christian faith was to risk superficiality or worse. Nevertheless, it seemed to me an opportunity too great to be missed. I decided that as I had recited the Apostles' Creed for over sixty years it would be a test of what I myself understood by it and must not, in any case, be an exercise in dogmatic theology. I have to admit that to preach it in this way was certainly quite a dangerous thing to do, because there would always be theologically-minded critics to tell me that I had fallen into one heresy or another! However, that danger was far less than refusing to speak about what I believe the

Apostles' Creed to mean in terms of daily living. It was an attempt, therefore, to speak from the heart to the heart across all barriers of culture and of faith.

I had no intention of publishing these addresses until I was told by the BBC that many requests had come in from all over the world for a record of what I had said. Hence, this small book.

I can only hope that with all its blemishes (of which I am only too well aware) it may help the kind of people who wrote to ask for a more permanent record.

I must thank, above all others, Miss Pauline Webb, who pressed me to undertake this venture, and also her most patient assistants in the World Service.

Introduction

I suppose that if you were to ask any Christian (except a Priest or Bishop) to say the Creed, he would find it quite difficult.

But if you asked him, or her, the simple question, "What do Christians believe?", he would find it even more difficult. There seem to be so many different things which make up the whole story of our Christian faith and our Christian life.

Looked at in one way we could say that Christians must obey the two great commandments: to love God with all our heart and soul and mind and strength, and our neighbour as ourself. That is certainly the way in which Christian life and behaviour are demonstrated. But looked at in another way, we could say that Christian faith depends on knowing God's word – on reading the Scriptures, the Old and New Testaments – on understanding what God is saying to us in the Bible.

In yet another way we could say that Christianity depends on **prayer** and **worship** – what we call private prayer and public worship. Without talking to God and listening to God we can't know Him as a person at all.

11

And most Christians would certainly say that in order to express our Christian faith we need to *share* it together, we need to belong to that community which is called "the Church". You can't live the Christian life as a solitary individual.

However, when we try to express all these different aspects of what we believe we find that each one of them leads us further, into yet more explanations; always, behind those explanations, is the further question: "But what makes Christianity different from other religions? What makes it unique?"

These are important questions. In our world, one of the most urgent tasks confronting humanity is the task of understanding one another. How can we hope for peace on earth if the great religions, Judaism, Islam, Buddhism, Christianity, and the rest — with their differing forms of worship and obedience to God — are all competing *against* one another? And we also know how, in the past, some of the worst and most bitter wars in history have been the religious wars. We must talk, we must have dialogue. But first and foremost, we must know how to express the meaning of our own faith.

It took three hundred years for the Christian Church to find a short way of defining, of making clear, what it believed about God, about Christ, about the Church — and about life itself. It was only as more and more people asked to be baptized, and therefore asked what they must believe *as Christians* that the Creed came to be written down. It was called "the Apostles' Creed", because it was originally thought to have been jointly composed by the twelve Apostles. It is that Creed that I want to look at, phrase by phrase, in this book.

1.
I Believe

These two words are expressed in one Latin word *credo* – from which our English word "creed" derives.

I think we have to be very clear about the meaning of the words "belief" and "believing" before we even begin to share together the great Christian truths we are called upon to believe in.

We live in a world in which science and technology have made such rapid and extraordinary advances that it almost seems as if they can explain everything. It seems as if the very meaning of life, its origins, its direction, its end, can be defined in scientific terms only. Examples are too numerous to mention more than a few. There is the adventure into space: men standing on the moon, men learning to live and move around for months away from Planet Earth. There are the discoveries in medical science known as "genetic engineering" – the control of life at its beginning, inside or outside the mother's womb. And, equally, there is the advance made in prolonging life beyond its natural terms . . . all the extraordinary experiments in heart transplants and their possibilities. There is the field of computer science and technology, which seems to be developing so fast that the idea of a "thinking" computer, able to produce its own solution to highly complex problems, is now not at all remote.

And – overshadowing them all – there is the consequence of nuclear fission and fusion, and the possible use of weapons which could totally destroy civilization if not humanity itself.

The consequence of all this is that human intelligence, the part of human nature which is used to study and to plan, the "reasoning" part of us, seems at the present time to have taken over control of human destiny. It can answer so many of the questions, can solve so many of the problems confronting us, that we ask, "Is there any limit to its capacity? Is there any mystery about life which it cannot solve?"

Yes, there is! And this mystery is the most fundamental one of all. It is posed for each of us as we go through this world . . . however much we may try to escape from it by busy-ness or activity; however often we push it out of our minds; however frequently we pretend it doesn't exist.

It is the question which lies at the heart of all human questions and of all religions: "What is life for?"

That question cannot be answered now by the reason or the intellect alone – and it never will be. It can only be answered by faith. That is to say, by belief in the One who stands over against the world; who, as all the great religions affirm, is Himself the meaning for the world's existence. The Christian Creed – the "I BELIEVE" of our religion – is an attempt, not to explain the mystery (for that is impossible) but to give us a statement which will both meet our bewilderment and yet hold us surely in truth.

2.
I Believe in God

Over twenty years ago there appeared in England a book called *God of a Hundred Names*, and in its preface the following words occur:

> From amidst diversified and often warring creeds: over a vast span of history: in the language of many a tribe and many a nation: out of the mouths of the learned and simple, the lowly and great: despite oceans of bloodshed and torturing inhumanities, and persecutions unspeakable – the single voice of a greater humanity rises confidently to heaven, saying "We adore Thee, who art One and who art Love: and it is in unity and love that we would live together, doing Thy will." If those who have heard this voice in their own hearts would be resolutely true to it . . . then indeed would our darkness be lightened, and the world's poisoned water be turned to wine.

(*God of a Hundred Names*, edited by Barbara Greene and Victor Gollancz; Gollancz, 1962).

I believe in GOD.

That is the tremendous statement with which the Christian Creed begins – and it is a statement that can be made not only by Christians but by the followers of all the great religions of the world, by whatever name they call Him. And the first thing to be said about the Creed is that, in its opening words, it affirms what the majority of the human race still accepts as the primal answer to the question "What is life for?" Life is for GOD.

It is surely important to get our religious perspectives right, yet it isn't always easy to do so, because religious language and religious terms seem to stand apart from our ordinary, everyday life. This is true even of the word "God". And, in fact, the writers of the Old Testament always remind us that God – by His very nature, just because He is God – is indescribable. They tell us of people who have known God in certain moments, and whose knowledge of Him is so deep that it is best described in events or symbols.

There is the lovely story of Jacob's dream of "a ladder set up on earth and the top of it reached to heaven and the angels of God were ascending and descending on it . . . and behold the Lord stood above it and said 'I am the Lord, the God of Abraham, your father' . . ." Or the story of Moses finding the bush that burnt yet was not consumed, and Moses said, "I will turn aside . . ." and God called him and said, "I am the God of your father . . . I will send you to Pharaoh." And in the course of that encounter came those strange words that

God said to Moses, "I am who I am" . . . Or Elijah on Mount Horeb, where the Lord was not in the wind or in the earthquake or in the fire but was "a still small voice" . . .

So, to say "I believe in God" is to make a statement whose truth can never be physically demonstrated, as a scientist would demonstrate the truth he wishes to express.

This is not because the existence of God is not real, but it is because God is God – beyond any human words or human thoughts or human actions: "No man has seen God at any time."

"In the beginning – GOD."

3.
The Father Almighty

Considering again the opening words of the Apostles' Creed – "I believe in God . . ." – we are reminded that, in a world like ours, dominated by the scientific and technological achievements of humanity, it is of first importance to understand what belief is . . . over against the demonstration of a scientific truth. This is not because belief is contrary to reason; it is not because faith is in opposition to intelligence, but simply because God is God and cannot be defined, cannot be known in human terms.

But now we come to a statement which seems to contradict all that. Here we are taught to think of God as "The Father" . . . and we all know what the word "Father" means. It is a familiar enough description for every human being. And it isn't too difficult, either, in using that word "Father" to enlarge and strengthen it in reference to God by adding the word "Almighty".

If you are like me, however, phrases such as

19

"Almighty God", "Almighty Father", are so much a part of our public worship in the prayers we say and the hymns we sing that we don't often stop to ponder or meditate about what they mean. Years ago, talking to a group of young boys in Sunday School class, I tried to discover what they thought God was like, how they imagined Him. One of them put up his hand and said, "He's like an old man with a beard!" ("More like a grandfather than a father") and clearly he had obtained his idea of God from a stained glass window trying to depict the impossible.

But what, truly, does this first statement in the Creed seek to tell us about the nature of God and why? It is a very necessary reminder that although *all* human language is totally inadequate to describe the nature of God, we have to use human language in order to make communication with God possible. And when Jesus was asked by His friends to teach them to pray, He Himself said, "When you pray say 'Our Father . . .'" And Jesus was using the word which runs through holy Scripture, in prophecy and psalm, in law and parable. Some of the most beautiful passages in both Old and New Testaments – and some of the most familiar – fill our minds with that imagery. Sometimes God is the father of His people, as in that beautiful verse in Hosea: "When Israel was a child, I loved him and out of Egypt I called my son . . ." Sometimes God is the father of the individual, nowhere more perfectly portrayed than in the parable of the Prodigal Son: "When he was yet a great way off his father saw him and ran and fell on his neck and kissed him . . ."

Always it is a picture of Love. And always too a picture of Love Almighty. Let us keep those two words together and not try to separate one from the other. The Almightiness of God our father is – as St John expressed it – "Herein is Love, NOT that we loved God but that He loved us."

Think of that Almighty Love when you say the first words of the Creed.

4.
Creator of Heaven and Earth

The Creed reminds us that God, whom we are to think of as "Father Almighty", is also Creator of Heaven and Earth.

In this the Creed simply states in a short phrase the first words of the first book of the Bible: "In the beginning God created the heavens and the earth" and, after the wonderful description of that act of creation, the writer of the Book of Genesis adds, "and God saw everything that he had made, and behold, it was *very good*".

Stated quite simply, as it is, this definition of God as Creator is of supreme importance to our whole life as Christians. Moreover it carries within itself a truth which the human race desperately needs to hear and to understand today. In fact we might say that it carries within itself three great truths by which as Christians we are bound to live.

First, that the world we live in is God's world, not

ours. Secondly, that the whole universe of which it is a tiny part is God's universe, not ours. And, finally, that if God is our Creator, we are His creatures – absolutely dependent on Him for every moment of our being. So that if He were to withdraw His creative presence for a millionth part of a second, we should cease to be. Such an obvious truth is so important to humanity today, because we are so proud of our scientific skills and our technological inventiveness; so greedy in our determination to use the marvellous richness of Planet Earth for our own ends; so determined to assert our own nationalisms and racialisms and cultures over against those of other people that we in fact forget that we are all *creatures*. We forget that this world is God's world, created and sustained by Him, and not ours "to do with it what we like".

This truth was brought home to me when I was visiting a small village in the South of Tanzania. It was evening, and round my hut gathered a group of small African children, under the African sky. I switched on my transistor radio for their enjoyment. The first voice to reach me was the voice of a Russian astronaut! The children asked me in Swahili, "Who is that? What is he doing?" All I could think of to say was, "He is a *man*!" Not a very profound remark, you might think!

But, in fact, it was one of the profoundest remarks I have ever made. For it was **Man** out there in space, looking down on Planet Earth – not on Russia or India, not on Africa or China – but on that little round globe. And he was saying "That's where I belong! That's home!"

23

If it is "God the Father Almighty" in whom we believe; if it is "God the Creator of Heaven and Earth" in whom we believe; if this marvellous world and everything in it is His creation and if each one of us is His creature – then we have this tremendous responsibility to live in and use what God has created and sustains for His glory and not for our own.

We must recover, before it is too late, the Christian doctrine of Creation. And we must also remember that God is the Creator of Heaven and Earth . . . that our Heaven is a Heaven not just of a myriad stars and planets and galaxies, but a Heaven for the glory of God to all eternity.

5.
I Believe in
Jesus Christ

We have examined and reflected on the first part of the Creed, on the great affirmation of belief in God as Father, as Love Almighty, as Creator and sustainer of the world and the universe. All of this section of the Christian creed is also acceptable to Judaism and Islam and, for the most part, to the other great world religions.

But now we come to the second great affirmation – I believe in Jesus Christ – and to the particular, and indeed unique, claims that Christians make about Him. We could say that this is the heart of the matter – the challenge, if you like, of Christianity itself – that which immediately differentiates it from the other world religions and demands both explanation and justification from those who claim the name of Christian. Indeed it is this part of the Creed which has been called by theologians "the scandal of particularity", and so it is – using "scandal" in the Greek sense of the word, "a stumbling-block" . . . an unexpected and therefore upsetting contradiction of what, until now, has appeared to be a religion acceptable to the whole human family. We have to decide whether it can be possible to say "I believe in God" and to know what we mean by such belief and total commitment, and then, using exactly that same word *credo*, "I believe", to say that we believe in a person, Jesus, who was born nearly two thousand years ago in a small village in the Middle East; who lived for some thirty-three years; and the record of whose life has been preserved for us . . . a historical person, in other words.

Is it really possible to believe in GOD – the indescribable, the infinite, the almighty – and to believe in Jesus Christ, someone very clearly described, whose life on earth was certainly finite (and very short) and who, in the whole manner of His life and death, did not *appear* to be almighty?

These are real questions. And when we say, "I believe in Jesus Christ", we must be prepared to answer them – not only when "outsiders" challenge us, but, much more importantly, when doubts and questions arise (as they surely must) in our own hearts.

Do we believe *in* Jesus Christ? The question is not, Do we believe *that* Jesus Christ existed? Or, Was he a good man, a healer, a teacher, a leader, a friend, a person of universal compassion and all-embracing love? We have to remember that we are using the words "believe in" – as we have used them of God.

We must think deeply about this part of the Creed,

but let us begin with the words themselves, "I believe in Jesus Christ" . . .

Jesus is not an uncommon name amongst the Jewish community – in fact the same as Joshua, the great successor to Moses. And, like all names in their origin, it has some kind of a meaning: "You shall call his name Jesus, for he will *save* his people from their sins". JESUS – SAVIOUR.

Christ. This is a Greek word meaning "The anointed One", and its Hebrew equivalent is **Messiah**, meaning the same thing – the one who is the expected saviour and deliverer of his people from oppression.

It is this *one* – Jesus Christ, Saviour, Deliverer – set apart, His uniqueness signified by His anointing, whom we say we *believe in*. Do we?

6.
His only Son

At every fresh statement of our Creed – our *credo*, our "I believe" – we need to stop and remember one thing. It is that the language of the Creed is *human* language, but the truth that the Creed is trying to express is *divine*, God-given truth. In other words there is always an impossibility, always a mystery (in the true sense of that word) which lies beyond reason and which words can never reach. The best we can do is to use familiar, everyday, universally understood language – words such as "father" or "son". "I believe in Jesus Christ, His *only* son . . ."

But it is also important to remember that the words of the Creed are not just one person's "bright idea". All of them are the result of over three hundred years of living the Christian life; sharing that experience; testing out the Gospel against everyday reality. And *then* trying to find the words which will express as accurately as possible the truth that has given birth to Christianity and to the Church.

There is a further authority to which to appeal: the authority of Jesus Christ Himself as He is shown to us in the written account of His life in the New Testament – and particularly in the four Gospels and in the Letters of St Paul and St John. Across the centuries Christians have heard the words of Jesus read out to them in their eucharistic worship; commented on in sermons and addresses; argued about by their teachers; written about by their theologians and scholars.

Therefore, when we come to the phrase "Jesus Christ, *His only son*", we have all that long and developing history behind us. And what we are saying, in fact, is that Jesus *is* the Son of God.

But does that get us much further? Isn't it true that if we believe in God as Father then all human beings are the children of God? What is the difference between Jesus and the rest of us? Well – that little word "only" (or "only begotten") is put there to remind us that we believe Jesus Christ to be the Son of God in a unique sense. And we say this because the Gospels themselves say it.

They say it in those lovely words, recorded by St Luke, as the message of the Archangel Gabriel to Mary, the Virgin:

"The Holy Spirit will come upon you and the power of the Most High will overshadow you, therefore the child to be born will be called holy, the Son of God."

They say it in the words of Jesus Himself as a child in the Temple at Jerusalem:

"Did you not know that I must be *in my Father's house*",

or in the week before He died, to a great crowd in Bethany:

"I have not spoken on my own authority, the Father who sent me has himself given me commandment what to speak . . ."

And on the very night before He died (in the words of St John):

Jesus, knowing that the Father had given *all* things unto his hand, and that he had come from God and was going to God . . .

Or – if you prefer the simplest statement of all – look at the first verse of St Mark's Gospel:

The beginning of the Gospel of Jesus Christ, the Son of God.

No. There can be no positive doubt that the words of the Creed are as perfect a summary as can be found of what Christians have ALWAYS believed about Jesus Christ. He is God's only Son.

7.
Our Lord

One of the characteristics of Jesus of Nazareth was very quickly recognized by His contemporaries, whether they were friendly or hostile: He had an extraordinary authority about Him. And it was an authority that did not appear to be *derived* – as it was in the case of, for example, the rulers of the country, who represented the Roman Emperor and the might of that empire itself. Nor was it, in the sphere of religion, the kind of authority which came from being a teacher of God's Law or a representative of the Levitical priesthood. "This man", they said, after his first sermon in the synagogue at Capernaum, "speaks with authority, and not as the scribes."

All through the descriptions of the ministry of Jesus given to us in the Gospels, the same note is struck. People come flooding to Him for healing – such a diversity of people, individuals like blind Bartimaeus, or the unknown woman with the issue of blood, or the

Roman soldier who is seeking healing for his own servant. In each case it is just a word or a touch or an assurance; and in each case it is an assertion or demonstration of authority – the self-authenticating authority of one who has no fear or doubt concerning the source of His own power. It is in particular an authority to call men and women out of their own way of life and into the way of life which is called "discipleship" – a following of Jesus Himself wherever He would have them go. "Follow me", he says – and immediately Simon and Andrew, and James and John leave their nets and their boats and follow Him. "He saw a man called Matthew sitting at the tax office and he said to him 'Follow me'. And he rose and followed Him." And that nice rich young man at the cross-roads, asking the question, "What must I do . . . with my life and my gifts and my opportunities?" . . . and the immediately disconcerting reply: "Go . . . sell . . . follow me."

It was an authority Jesus constantly used as a challenge – a challenge to all who questioned His right to forgive sin. It was at this level, more than in any other way, that He ran into conflict with the religious leaders of His day. To the paralysed man, let down through the roof of a house, He says, "My son, your sins are forgiven", and those sitting around "questioning in their hearts" say, "Who can forgive sins but God alone?" Jesus, we are told, said to them, "Which is easier, to say 'Your sins are forgiven' or to say 'Rise, take up your bed and walk'?", and He said just that. And when the paralysed man got up and walked they said, "We never saw anything like this."

It is the absolute authority of Jesus which causes His disciples to call Him "Lord". That applies not only to the disciples who actually heard Him teach, who watched His acts of healing, who saw Him "with publicans and sinners" bringing to them the joy and forgiveness of a new life. But it applies also to all the millions of us, through the centuries, who have known His authority in our own lives; who cannot find any other title to call Him but "Lord" . . . OUR Lord.

But then we read His warning against using words without meaning them. "You call me Master and Lord . . . and you say well, for so I am. If I, your Lord and Master, have washed your feet, you must wash one another's feet. A servant is not greater than his master, nor is he who is sent greater than he who sent him."

We are a "servant Church". Our authority, both corporately and individually, will depend upon whether we really live this truth.

8.
Who was conceived by the Holy Ghost

We live – as we have already noticed – in an age which is dominated by a scientific world view.

This is not at all surprising when we look around us at the achievements of science and technology in so many areas of human life. In fact we know that the pace of scientific discovery has outstripped our capability to provide moral and ethical response to it. This is particularly the case with medical science and with those discoveries in genetics which have such frightening possibilities for the future of humanity. It is, literally, the matters of life and death now so powerfully affected by the fantastically rapid advance in medical research, and their immediate application to human problems, that have created this new atmosphere surrounding conception and childbirth.

I am fully aware of these issues; or at least, as fully

aware as an ordinary person without medical or scientific expertise can ever be. I know that there are universally complex problems concerning the moments after conception, and all the new knowledge of possible abnormalities which is available to us. In common with millions of others, I have heard the arguments for and against abortion; for and against contraception; for and against artificial insemination, test-tube babies, in vitro fertilization and "surrogate mothers" . . . And I fully recognize that it *is* the duty of the Christian Church (and indeed of all the world religions) to give some guidance, to speak with real knowledge and authority, on such matters. For all of this is related to the great fact upon which our faith rests. The fact that God has taken our human nature to Himself; has shared our human life, from the cradle to the grave and beyond the grave; and has therefore given to that human nature an infinite and eternal dignity. God – we say – has "become Man". "The Word was made flesh and dwelt among us."

It is this that we are talking about when we use the word "Incarnation", the "En-fleshment" of God. "Who was conceived . . ." But then: "Who was conceived by the Holy Ghost."

Once again the Creed is trying to convey in the shortest possible phraseology – in only seven words, in fact – what is told us at great length and in marvellous poetry by St Luke – what is told us in much more philosophical language by St John – what is taken for granted in the writings of St Paul – and what has been the faith of ordinary, non-theological, non-philosophical, non-poetic Christians all through the ages. This, yet again, is something where human language struggles to reach out into a deep mystery, the mystery of God Himself.

In fact, it is not attempting in any way to express the truth scientifically; for it is a truth that cannot be expressed in that way. It is a truth which can only be apprehended by **faith** – but it is no less true for that reason. Indeed, it is much more true for that reason because it is an expression of God's love for humankind, for you and me, with all our weakness and ignorance and fear – a love which can carry us through even the darkest passages of our journey through life.

"Conceived by the Holy Ghost" . . . "Do not be afraid Mary ["Fear not" – the favourite words of Jesus] you have found favour with God . . . the Holy Spirit will come upon you, and the power of the Most High will overshadow you, therefore the child to be born will be called holy, the Son of God."

9.
Born of the Virgin Mary

"The Blessed Virgin Mary." Such a familiar name to so many millions; such an extraordinary title of honour to give to one individual. All over the world it is the source of the most reverent devotion and piety, as well as the first name for girls, whether they be princesses, or film-stars, barmaids or journalists . . . Mary – or, quite simply, "The Blessed Virgin".

There can be no doubt that both the person and her title have inspired some of the greatest works of art ever painted, ever carved in stone or wood, ever displayed in great Byzantine ceilings, or ancient, glowing ikons.

Yet, at the same time, touchingly tawdry, sentimental, mass-produced statuettes of Mary have the place of honour in churches and private prayer-corners all over the world. Famous shrines and centres of pilgrimage, like Lourdes or Loreto or Walsingham, continue to draw millions of Christians, as they have done through the centuries.

It is as impossible to think of Christianity without the Blessed Virgin Mary as it is to think of it without the risen, ascended and glorified Christ Himself.

And this article of the Creed, this statement of our belief, explains why. We believe in "Jesus Christ God's only son our Lord . . . conceived by the Holy Ghost, *born of the Virgin Mary*."

However many theologians, through the ages, have attempted to explain, or to explain away, the "Virgin birth", it still remains at the very heart and centre of our faith. Indeed it is also at the very heart and centre of the mystery of the Christian Gospel itself. That impossible paradox which is called the Incarnation, the "En-fleshment" of God, God so identifying Himself with humanity that He *has* to enter His world as every other human being enters His world – by being born.

But why is it necessary for Him to be born "of a virgin"? Doesn't this make it extraordinarily difficult to give honour to marriage and to motherhood itself? If – say the critics of Christianity – you so exalt the state of virginity, don't you at the same time diminish the state of matrimony? Are you not in danger of promoting one of the most dangerous heresies – the heresy of the Manichee, which in fact would have us believe that the flesh itself, that human nature itself, is somehow evil?

Certainly these arguments, in one way or another, have appeared throughout Christian history. Certainly the charge of "mariolatry" – the worship of Mary –

has been levelled often enough at those who have a devotion to the Blessed Virgin, sometimes with appalling consequences in religious conflict.

Yet the story of the conception and birth of Jesus, as presented in the two Gospels that record these events, is unequivocal: this young virgin – they state – is the mother of God. The Creed and the Gospel are at one in their unbelievable assertion: virgin *and* Mother. It is unbelievable, yet believed. It is impossible, yet taken right into the whole Christian tradition. Somehow we can only understand the absolute uniqueness of one who is both fully God and fully Man in the absolute uniqueness of His birth – and therefore in the absolute uniqueness of His Mother Mary.

10.
Suffered under Pontius Pilate

How quickly we can say those words. And how often in our life have we said them without a thought about their true meaning! Just as, perhaps, walking through a cemetery or a churchyard, we see a name on a grave; the date of birth; the date of death and the familiar words "Rest in Peace". Yet at some time that name and that inscription were put there by a son or a daughter, a husband or a wife, with great love. Those simple words were so much more than just words recording an event. They summed up the meaning of a whole life.

The trouble with the words of the Creed is that they are meant for one purpose only: to state as simply and clearly as possible those beliefs which all Christians everywhere accept and profess as the basis of their religion. Yet they have to be expressed in such a way that they can be used without lengthy explanations. After all, in one form or another, the Creed was and is used at baptism, the public occasion, the sacrament when the Christian life begins and the child of God enters the family of God which we call the Church.

"He suffered under Pontius Pilate." Such a short statement in the Creed! Yet, if you look at the four Gospels in the New Testament, the events which those words describe take up more space than the descriptions of any other part of the life and teaching and ministry of Jesus – in St John's Gospel three whole chapters, in St Mark, St Matthew and St Luke, two. And that is without mentioning the constant references in St Paul's letters to that which he describes as glory . . . "glory in the Cross of our Lord Jesus Christ".

Not to mention, either, throughout the whole length of Christian history – in the writings of every theologian and every saint, in the painting of every great artist, in the music of so many of the greatest composers – the Passion of Our Lord Jesus Christ: "the things that He suffered" upon which our minds and hearts are fixed.

So come back again to those words of the Creed, and pause for a moment to think why they are of such overwhelming meaning and significance to us today.

"He suffered." Who suffered? Already in the Creed we have expressed our belief that Jesus Christ is the Son of God "conceived by the Holy Ghost, born of the Virgin Mary". And it is on the basis of that faith that we go on to say, "He suffered." For me it is those two words which make Christianity a possible religion for humanity at all. For me, if the God I worship is *only* a God "out beyond the shining of the farthest star', then I do not care to worship Him at all. Because one thing I

41

do know about human life in this world is that pain and suffering, sorrow and loneliness are inescapably a part of it, and in today's turbulent world these things are shown and shared more completely than ever before in human history. The hunger, the homelessness, the violence, the terror we see on our television screens are inescapable. But our God – the God we worship – has come into this kind of world: He knows all about it from within: He shares the pain with us. And that for only one reason: Love.

Pontius Pilate – the representative of the great Empire of Rome at a particular moment in history – reminds us that the Passion, the sufferings of Christ, are real, they are historical events, not illusion.

So our faith can be real too, not a myth, but a truth to live by.

11.
Was crucified, dead and buried

No generation in the whole history of the human family has known more about the reality of violent and horrible death than our own. Is that an exaggeration? I do not think so.

In the first place, the very fact of mass communication by radio and television is new to mankind. For the first time it is possible to see death in war, in acts of terror, in the famine areas of the world, *as it happens*. It is there in our sitting room, even if we can't stretch out our hand to touch, to relieve the pain of the dying; even if we can't speak a word of comfort to the bereaved woman with the dead child in her arms.

But it is not only the capability to be a participant or an onlooker, it is also the fact that our generation has lived through seventy years (a human life-time in biblical terms) of unceasing war. Two 'World Wars' have involved virtually every corner of the globe, resulting, in each case, in the slaughter of millions. In the continuing conflicts after the Second World War more and yet more terrible weapons of destruction have been deployed and more and more innocent lives have been caught up: the lives of civilians quite remote from the fighting, the lives of small children and old women have been lost; the lives of those who had no opportunity to choose their future in God's world have been thrown away like worthless rubbish. But war – that ultimate decision by human beings and their nations to call death to their aid – is not the only cause of death. There are also the so-called "natural disasters" of famine or flood – in our generation affecting so many millions more than in the past, because of the vast increase in population on this small Planet Earth which is our home.

"He was crucified, dead and buried." Stop and think for a moment about that word "crucified". We Christians certainly need to do that because so many of our hymns and prayers use it, and because we have been so accustomed to the crosses on our buildings or our altars that we have forgotten what crucifixion really was. Yet even with our knowledge of the horrors of modern instruments of torture and death it is hard to conceive of a worse torture, a worse death, than being nailed to a cross and left to die – slowly, in tormenting thirst and weakness and agony before a mocking crowd. Jesus was crucified. He knew the agony of death at its very worst. He cried out in the darkness, "My God, my God, why hast thou forsaken me?" And so he is a God who knows from experience the ultimate, absolute bitterness of death, for He has shared it.

In that unspeakable horror of the concentration camps set up by Hitler, where six million Jews and other opponents of Nazism were deliberately killed, one victim was a thirteen-year-old Polish boy. He was hanged upon a gallows with two adults. Here is the description of his death by an eye-witness.

"Long live liberty!" they cried. But the child was silent. "Where is God? Where is He?" someone behind asked. At a sign from the head of the camp the three chairs tipped over. The crowd was ordered to march past the gallows. The two adults were no longer alive. But the third rope was still moving: being so light, the child was still alive. Behind me I heard the same man asking, "Where is God now?" And I heard a voice within me answer him, "Where is He? Here He is – He is hanging here on this gallows."

12.
He descended into Hell

The previous words of the Apostles' Creed were clear in their meaning; there was no doubt at all: "He was crucified, dead and buried." In the Gospel story itself, and in all the difficult and controversial comments on it through the centuries, there has never been any doubt or difficulty about those words at all.

But when we come to the statement (as it is used in English in the Book of Common Prayer) "He descended into Hell", there we do need to ask ourselves some questions. Very many Christians say these words without really understanding what they mean. And in a sense, as with so many other great truths of the Christian faith, it is simply the case that human language is just not adequate to express such truths.

One difficulty can be easily disposed of, and in modern English translations and languages other than English, this has already been done. In this clause of the Apostles' Creed "Hell" does not mean the place of torment and damnation, where "the worm dieth not and the fire is not quenched", but quite simply it means "the place of the departed". In fact it could better be translated: "He descended to the Dead".

But even then, questions arise. Who are the dead to whom Jesus "descends"? Why does He visit them? One of the most important tasks for anyone interpreting the Creed is to look to Holy Scripture and see where – if anywhere – such statements originate. For it is only in the Bible that we can look with confidence for an explanation.

In the first letter of Peter there is what seems to have been a kind of hymn, and in the middle of it are these words: "Christ died for sin once for all, the righteous for the unrighteous, *that he might bring us to God*, being put to death in the flesh but made alive in the spirit *in which he went and preached to the spirits in prison*."

The hymn goes on to link this mysterious visit with baptism, as if to say that Christ, having conquered death Himself, *must* bring the fruits of that victory to those who, being faithful to God (like Noah and his companions), *must* find a place within the family of believers. It is as if Peter is saying, "The good news of the victory over *all* the powers of darkness must be proclaimed at once to those who are still suffering the consequences of the power of evil in the world." In other words *all* "the dead", all those who have lived in God's world before the coming of His Son, must share in the joy of being able to repent, together with those who have heard the Gospel proclaimed in life.

So it is traditional to think of those days between Good Friday and Easter Sunday – the days when, as it were, nothing happens – as the days when Christ is visiting the spirits in prison and setting them free. Of course it is "a mystery" in the true sense of the word; something inexpressible because it is beyond the reach of human language. Yet it tells the same truth as those marvellous words of St Paul:

Who shall separate us from the love of Christ? I am sure that neither death, nor life, nor angels, nor principalities, nor things present, nor things to come, nor powers, nor height, nor depth, nor anything else in all creation, will be able to separate us from the love of God in Christ Jesus our Lord.

13.
The Third Day He rose again from the Dead

On one of his pastoral visits a few years ago, the present Pope, speaking to the vast crowd who had come to welcome him, said, "WE are the Easter people!"

There is no simpler or better description of what it means to be a Christian than that. We *are* the Easter people because, as St Paul tells us very clearly and firmly, "If Christ has not been raised, then our preaching is in vain [is worthless] and your faith is in vain."

And so at the heart of the Creed there is that simple affirmation: "The Third Day He rose again from the dead." Nobody *saw* the event we call "the Resurrection", so it is for ever impossible to describe how it happened. A few people (those closest to Jesus during His ministry and in His last hours before He died on the Cross) saw His tomb empty and the grave-clothes lying empty too. Many more people – single or in larger groups – saw Jesus after He was risen, heard His voice, touched Him, walked with Him, even ate with Him. And one in particular, Saul "the persecutor", who had never seen him in the flesh, wrote those very words: "If Christ has not been raised, then our preaching is in vain" . . . and so is your faith.

But there is a question we need to ask ourselves – not only on Easter Sunday, not only when we say the Creed or join in the Eucharist or end our prayers with words like "through Jesus Christ our Lord, *who is alive and reigns* for ever and ever", but at other times too. We must ask it at those times when religion seems to have nothing to do with our ordinary daily life, to bring us comfort or help strong enough to break through the dark hours of pain, bereavement or loneliness. The question we need to ask ourselves is: What would my religion mean to me *without* the Resurrection? Archbishop Michael Ramsey answers:

> Everywhere in the New Testament writings the event is referred to NOT as Jesus *rising* but as Jesus *being raised*, as God raising Him. It was a mighty act of God . . . when things are down and out God acts. When things are dark, when life is dead, when human possibilities are exhausted, God acts. It is that which colours the whole Christian idea of faith. You do not consciously grow better and better. You find yourself down and out in the confusion of guilt and failure: God acts, and the self that was broken is the self restored, with a new centre that the self could not devise.

So Jesus lives!

We come to the garden on that first Easter morning, and Mary Magdalene has been there much earlier, "while it was still dark". All she can think of, as she sees that the stone at the entrance to the tomb has been taken away, is that Christ's body has been taken too, she tells Peter and John.

But she stays near the tomb, weeping. It is her tears that blind her so that she sees, but does not see, Jesus standing close to her.

Supposing him to be the gardener she says, "Sir, if you have carried him away tell me." Jesus said to her, "Mary!"

That is the reality of the Resurrection. It is the deepest meaning of the whole Christian faith. It is that which has sustained the Church through all the centuries. The Lord calls us – each one of us – by name, and we reply with Mary, "Master!"

HE IS RISEN!
HE LIVES!
WE LIVE BY HIS LIFE.

14.
He ascended into Heaven

Most of us will remember that exciting day, not so many years ago, when Yuri Gagarin, the Russian astronaut, became the first human being to enter space and circle Planet Earth. Since those days of wonder much has happened in space, and still continues to happen, that will have enormous consequences for humanity. We are perhaps more conscious now of fear than of exhilaration, particularly as we are faced with the so-called "Star Wars" research programme. As with so many other happenings in our world, a sign of hope has become a sign of bewilderment, as the complexity of the choices now open to us through scientific and technological discovery increases.

In fact that great adventure of Yuri Gagarin was greeted by the then head of government in the Soviet Union – Mr Khrushchev – with a cynical remark to the effect that, "There was no report of finding God up there in Heaven!" Of course Mr Khrushchev knew very well that he was not attacking the reality of Christian belief as it is expressed in this clause of the Creed, "He *ascended* into Heaven". He had, after all, been born into the Russian Orthodox Church and, like Stalin before him, he knew (even if he rejected) the theological truths held by Christians through the centuries. He was simply using the great event of the venture into space as a kind of assertion of materialism and its philosophy, over against the childishness, the superstition, the ignorance of all who still cling to religion. And he used the Ascension as a useful stick to beat the Christians with.

These developments are yet another reason why Christians should think again about the meaning of those beliefs we so frequently profess but so often hand over to others as being too difficult, too mysterious to explain to our non-believing contemporaries – or even to our own children! The word "Ascension" is the cause of the trouble, because, in this space age, we are constantly hearing it used. Even in the ordinary, familiar, context of air travel we hear the pilot announcing, "We shall ascend to 30,000 feet . . ." But the Ascension of Jesus into Heaven does not mean, and was never understood to mean, that Heaven is a place "above the bright blue sky". **Heaven is where God is**. And just as we believe, with St Paul, that "He ascended" means "He had also descended" – to that bare stable at Bethlehem and to that mysterious region of the departed – so we believe (again in St Paul's words) that "He ascended above all the heavens, that

53

He might free all creatures." What a claim! We are caught once again in the ever-present difficulty of using human language to express the inexpressible divine truth. As the good historian he was, St Luke had to state that there came a moment in the life of Jesus when His mission in this world was complete and perfect. The "Ascension" (not His death on the cross, nor even His resurrection on the third day) marks the fulfilment of His mission. But to the Christian Church it could not mean, and in all the centuries never meant, that Jesus had been born, had lived, had died – and had left them only a memory.

There had to be a moment when the change from a knowledge of His physical presence became the sure and certain knowledge of His abiding spiritual presence, known by faith only in the heart and soul, but proved a million times over by the existence, the continuance, the world-wide mission of this Church.

JESUS LIVES!
JESUS IS GLORIFIED!

15.
He sitteth on the right hand of God

We have already noticed more than once the absolute impossibility of using human language to describe the great mysteries of the Christian faith. All we can do is to use very familiar, everyday words as symbols or signs of what we really want to express. We want to say something which will convey the truth of Christ's triumphant and glorious existence in Heaven after His Passion, His death, and His resurrection. And so in the Creed we affirm this belief by the simplest possible words: "He sits on the right hand of God."

Heaven is where God is: Christ is in Heaven: Christ is in glory. What else can be said?

This could be yet another part of the Christian Creed that is, as it were, pure theology – in the sense that though we believe it to be true it doesn't appear to have much relevance to where we are now: to our daily life in this turbulent old world of ours. In fact, it might even be used by our opponents to justify Marx's saying that "religion is the opium of the people". For if the Master we serve, having been born and lived and shared our humanity from the cradle to the grave, has now removed Himself from this "vale of tears" and returned to Heaven, what has been the use of it all? He is so remote, so far "out beyond the shining of the farthest star", that He is irrelevant.

Of course Karl Marx meant more than this. He meant that society in this world needed radical change (revolution) if all were to be able to share in the earth's wealth and resources. He felt that this revolution, which would mean "each according to his ability, giving to each according to his need", was being fatally hindered by religion – for religion was telling men that, like Jesus Himself, they would one day come to the end of toil and hardship and be happy with God for ever in Heaven. Religion, and particularly the Jewish and Christian forms of religion, was the opium that transformed that dream into a present reality – fantasy though it was.

Unfortunately in the long history of the Christian Church this kind of presentation of Heaven as the alternative to earth has been only too common, particularly at those times when religious people themselves forget what they are taught to pray for: "Thy Kingdom come *on earth* as it is in Heaven". Christ "sitting on the right hand of God", Christ in Glory, so far from being remote from us has in fact "taken our manhood [that is, the humanity that He shares with us] *into* God."

So we have the picture of one who is in glory, but to

balance that picture and give it its significance and meaning, we might do worse than remember a line or two from the poet William Blake:

> I give you the end of a golden string
> Only wind it into a ball.
> It will bring you in at Heaven's gate
> Built in Jerusalem's wall.

We, too, are created for glory! Not for the kind of glory that is expressed so often in the triumphs and victories of armies or rulers here on earth, but for the kind of glory which Jesus promises as the reward of love. That "golden string" – which is the life of faith, lived out where we are, expressed by our common life in the Body of Christ, the Church – will certainly bring us in at Heaven's gate, will bring us home. And no one is wrong to look forward to getting home – least of all to hearing the Master say:

"Well done, good and faithful servant – enter into the joy of your Lord."

"At that day ye shall know that I am in the Father and ye in me and I in you."

So Christ, seated at the right hand of the Father, is the object not just of our praise and thanksgiving and joy, but of the contemplative prayer that sustains our Christian life on earth.

16.
From thence He shall come

It is not surprising that in a turbulent world like ours people should talk and write and produce films about "the End". Much of the science fiction that is so popular in the West is just another way of speaking about "the end of the world" – or at least of our world – in conflict with one of the myriad other worlds in space. And, indeed, it is understandable when we know that there are more than enough nuclear weapons to destroy Planet Earth twenty times over – and that yet more and more fearful ones are planned.

But in fact the Bible, in both the Old and New Testaments, has a lot to say about "the end of the age", not only in the book called The Apocalypse or Revelation of St John, but in many of the great prophets like Ezekiel, in the book of Daniel and in all the teachings about the Messiah, the Christ. There is always, too, a connection between that "coming" of the end of the age and "the One who shall come" to bring in the Kingdom, the Sovereignty of God. So it is not surprising that the Apostles' Creed – that affirmation of what Christians believe – speaks about it too. The phrase "Jesus . . . sitteth at the right hand of the Father" is linked with "From thence, *he shall come*".

What is known as "the Second Coming" of Christ is a truth that is part of the Gospel: part, in fact, of St Mark's Gospel, which most people believe to have been the earliest one written. "Truly, I say to you", said Jesus, "there are some standing here who will not taste death before they see the Kingdom of God come with power." That is a hard saying in itself. And here is another: "But in those days, after the tribulation the sun will be darkened . . . and the powers in the heavens will be shaken. And then they will see the Son of man *coming* in clouds with great power and glory . . ." So these verses (and others, like the one in St Paul's letter to the Church in Thessalonica, "For the Lord Himself will descend from Heaven with a cry of command . . . with the sound of the trumpet of God" . . .) are enough to show that the words in the Apostles' Creed are not science fiction, but are based on the teaching of Jesus Himself, and are meant to be taken seriously by all Christians. But how do they affect us here and now, in our day and generation?

In Christ's day and generation it was taken for granted that God would end what God alone had begun: that as the world's creation is God's work, so the world's dissolution and consummation is God's work too. ("In the beginning God" . . . and in the end God.)

But in the attempt to convey the meaning of such an end, all kinds of picture stories – "myths" we call them – were used.

St Mark devotes one whole chapter, the thirteenth, to the way in which Jesus used those picture stories to explain that great truth. Yes, He said, the Son of Man would come – they, His disciples, would see Him come (whether alive on earth or already part of the Church in paradise). But when His friends naturally asked Him "When?" He was very, very definite (and I suppose they were very, very disappointed!): "Of that day or that hour NO ONE KNOWS, not even the angels in heaven, NOR THE SON, but ONLY THE FATHER!" Yes, we believe that He will come, as the Christian Church has always believed. (The season we call Advent – "Coming" – four weeks before Christmas, is not only a preparation for His coming birth, but for His second coming in glory.) Yet that is not a reason for "putting off" our Christian responsibilities until He arrives. It is a reason – the only reason perhaps – for being TRULY AWAKE EVERY HOUR OF EVERY DAY!

"Watch therefore, for you do not know when the Master of the House will come – at evening, at midnight, at cockcrow, or in the morning."

DON'T LET HIM FIND YOU ASLEEP . . . WATCH!

17.
From thence He shall come to Judge

Some books are so unusual, or so beautifully written, that they stay in one's mind for ever. About eleven years ago I read such a book. It was called *Mister God, this is Anna*, and was the true story of a little girl called Anna who, before the Second World War, was one of the thousands of homeless children wandering the streets of London. She was found one night, dirty, hungry and cold, trying to get some warmth from the window of a baker's shop. The book is the story of three and a half years in which Fynn (her rescuer) came to know Anna and to love her. He kept a record of everything she said to him, because he realized that to Anna God was more real than anyone else, and because her love for "Mister God" (that was the way she always spoke of Him and spoke to Him) was so great. Anna died in one of those totally unexpected accidents, falling from a tree trying to rescue a pet kitten. But before she died, she said to her friend, "Fynn, I love you." "I love you too, Anna."

"Fynn, I bet Mister God lets me get into heaven for this."

Jesus told us all very plainly, that unless we can become like little children we cannot enter the Kingdom of Heaven. But I have told the story of Anna and of her certainty about getting into Heaven because it has a truth to tell us about one of the most difficult of all the articles of the Apostles' Creed. We should think carefully of it. "From thence", we say of Jesus, "He shall come to JUDGE . . ." Jesus as Judge is certainly not the Jesus most Christians like to think about unless they have to! Jesus as Friend, yes! Jesus as Saviour, yes! Jesus as Master and Lord, yes! But most of us prefer to leave to another time (our death-bed perhaps?) thoughts of Jesus as Judge.

When we were considering the "Coming" of Jesus, we saw that He Himself had warned us not to ask the question "When?"; "because of that day and hour no man knows, not even the Son, but the Father." But it is Jesus Himself who answers the question "Why?" Why does He come?

"When the Son of Man comes in His glory . . . then He will sit on His glorious throne. Before Him will be gathered all the nations and He will separate them one from another as a shepherd separates the sheep from the goats."

That is from St Matthew's Gospel, and here is St John:

"As the Father has life in Himself, so he has granted the Son also to have life in Himself and has given

62

Him authority to execute judgement because He is the Son of Man . . ."

In thinking of Judgement, therefore, the truth which, for Christians, must be the heart of the matter, is the truth that Jesus Himself will be the Judge. That same Jesus who has called us, whose disciples (however poor and feeble we are) we know ourselves to be; that same Jesus who "knew what was in man" and who knows what we are far better than we know ourselves; that same Jesus who loves each one "to the uttermost" . . . it is before Him that we shall stand. We *shall* stand? It is before Him that we *do* stand, every hour and every day of our lives.

Anna was right to have no fear; she was right to believe that she would go to Heaven. Not because there is *no* Judgement, but because the Judgement is in the hand of Him who says:

"Truly, truly, I say to you, the hour is coming and now is when the dead will hear the voice of the Son of God: AND THEY WHO HEAR WILL LIVE . . ."

18.
To Judge both the Quick [living] and the Dead

Of all the virtues that humanity can agree to be necessary for a good life here in this world, justice takes pride of place. John Rawles, a great modern philosopher, has put it like this: "Justice is the first virtue of social institutions, as truth is of systems of thought . . . laws and institutions no matter how efficient and well arranged must be reformed or abolished if they are unjust." And although it may be true that a Judge does not and cannot create justice in society, he bears a major responsibility for preserving it and so for preserving peace itself.

We know that "he who comes to judge" is, in Christian belief, our Lord Jesus Christ. Using His own words from the Gospel of St John, we recognize that we are not able to answer the question "*When* shall He come to judge us?", for "of that day and hour no man knows, not even the Son, but the Father".

In the clause from the Creed at the head of this

64

chapter we are told how He comes to judge, namely, that He judges "both the living and the dead". In other words, the justice which our Judge will dispense reaches the whole of humanity without partiality, prejudice or discrimination; it goes right across all the barriers of space and time – it is universal. And this, like so many other truths expressed in the Creed, is a deeply mysterious idea. Humanly speaking, it is beyond our understanding – or it would be if Christ did not Himself explain what it must mean.

As always, He began His explanation with a parable that everyone in His audience would understand:

"When the Son of man comes in his glory . . . before Him will be gathered all the nations, and He will separate them one from another *as a shepherd separates the sheep from the goats* . . ."

The people to whom He spoke had only to look at the hillside to see a shepherd bringing in from the common pasture those sheep and goats and then, before they entered the fold, separating them from each other. In the Palestine of Christ's day one of the commonest images was that of a king on his throne as the God of justice. Jesus is that King, that Judge, and He speaks to all those in front of Him as they await judgement. It is a familiar enough passage from St Matthew's Gospel, perhaps a little too familiar because, as with other parables and stories, we don't bother to read between the lines, we don't always catch the tone of voice in which Jesus speaks. But here are

His words:

> The King will say to those at his right hand [the
> sheep] "Come, O blessed of my Father, inherit the
> Kingdom prepared for you from the foundation of
> the world; for I was hungry and you gave me food, I
> was thirsty and you gave me drink, I was a stranger
> and you welcomed me, I was naked and you clothed
> me, I was sick and you visited me, I was in prison and
> you came to me."

And to their question, "When did all this happen," the
great reply:

> "Inasmuch as you did it to one of *the least of these my
> brethren*; you did it to ME."

But what about the others (the goats)?

> "Depart from me ye cursed . . . for I was hungry . . .
> thirsty . . . a stranger . . . sick . . . in prison . . . "

and the parallel question, "When?" with the parallel
answer:

> ". . . as you did it *not to one of the least of these you
> did it not to me*."

JUDGEMENT is given! JUSTICE is done!
Strangely, we are happy with this; somehow we just
can't imagine that we would be one of the goats, the
rejected, the lost-for-ever. This shows a deep truth
about human beings, wherever and whoever they are.
Secretly, in our deepest heart, we identify not with

those who stand in front of the Judge and are condemned, but with those, all white and clean like the sheep, who are *not*!

Sure of our own virtue, we have all the more need to listen to those other words of Christ: "JUDGE NOT, THAT YE BE NOT JUDGED!"

19.
I Believe in the
Holy Ghost

Even though everyone who recites the Apostles' Creed knows that the word "Ghost" is only an old English translation of the word "spirit", it does not help us very much. For the word "spirit" – *spiritus* in Latin or *pneuma* in Greek – only means "wind", and what do we understand by a "holy wind"? Once again we realize how impossible human language can be as a vehicle of God's truth. Yet it is all we have, and it is, in one way or another, all that Holy Scripture can find for the purpose, except, of course, for signs and symbols, of which there are many, and in particular those used to explain the work of the Holy Spirit.

Talking to Nicodemus about the "second birth" of baptism, Jesus said, "That which is born of flesh is flesh and that which is born of spirit is spirit." And He went on to say, "The *wind* [spirit] blows where it wills and you hear the sound of it, but you do not know whence it came from or whither it goes: so it is with everyone who is born of the spirit."

This is yet another of Jesus' parables from nature – just as the wind is free and invisible and unpredictable, so Christian rebirth is also free and invisible and unpredictable too. But it is an experience, a fact upon which a new life is built.

Sometimes the demands that Jesus made upon His friends, His closest disciples, seem unfair. He tells them, St John records, that they will have to face all kinds of tests – horrible tests, like being turned out of the synagogue (ostracism) and even facing death – and then He says: "Nevertheless I tell you the truth, it is to your advantage that I go away." How on earth could it be? He had chosen them, He had taught them, He had formed them into a fellowship which depended utterly on His leadership. And now He was going to leave them to face a totally hostile world, and He said, "It is expedient for you" – because if He didn't go away the Counsellor, the Advocate, the Strengthener, who is the Holy Spirit, would not come to them.

There are so many ways of trying to define the person of the Holy Spirit; so many ways of trying to define the work of the Holy Spirit; and His gifts to the Church; and His fruits in the lives of individuals; and His meaning for God's creation, God's world, God's purposes for the universe; so many ways that it is difficult to know where to begin or where to end.

A book written a few years ago by Bishop John Taylor has the title *The Go-Between God*, and it is a wonderful explanation of the Holy Spirit. But its title shows the difficulty confronting us as we say these words of the Creed. All we can say, all we can believe, comes from the certainty that it is the Holy Spirit who brings home to our heart the *certainty* of God's power, of God's love, of God's peace. All we can say is that – in the Church's witness to the truth of the Gospel through the centuries there has been a life-giving Spirit at work who fulfils completely the words that Jesus spoke of Him.

"When the spirit of *truth* comes He will guide you into all the truth . . . He will glorify Me, for He will take what is mine and declare it to you . . . All that the Father has is mine, therefore I said that He will take of mine and declare it to you." There is the Go-between God.

And still I haven't mentioned the day of Pentecost, when that little band of frightened men and women gathered all together in one place, "and suddenly a sound came from heaven *like the rush of a mighty wind* . . . and there appeared to them *tongues as of fire* [the best sign and symbol of the Love that purifies and warms and glows against the darkness] . . . and they were all filled with the Holy Spirit . . ."

And, without any power but His they "TURNED THE WORLD UPSIDE DOWN!"

20.
The Holy Catholic Church

Until this point in the Creed we have been expressing our faith in God – in His being, in His nature, in that most mysterious yet central truth for Christians which we call the Holy Trinity – and we have said that we believe in God the Father, God the Son and God the Holy Spirit.

But now we come down to earth! In these last clauses of the Creed we profess our faith in our own humanity as it is, as it is meant to be, as God intends and wills it to be here on earth and through all eternity.

We begin with "the Church", and we are told to call it HOLY and CATHOLIC. Remembering that we, you and I together with all Christians everywhere, are part of it – how can we possibly call it HOLY?

And remembering that the word CATHOLIC means "universal" – not only in the geographical sense of "world-wide", but in the historical sense of "always" throughout history, and in the popular sense of "all-inclusive" – how on earth can we use such a word at all? Isn't it obvious that there are still vast areas of the world which do not belong to the Christian Church? That through the past two thousand years Christianity as a world religion has been overtaken by cataclysmic world events and is still "tossed about by many a conflict, many a doubt" as it faces vast scientific, technological and ideological change? And – most and worst of all – remembering that the Church is deeply divided within itself as to what it believes. If it were not, we would not be involved so passionately in the ecumenical movement, the movement to express our Christian unity. If the Church were really HOLY AND CATHOLIC it would surely also be ONE?

What comes to mind when we use, or even hear, the word "church"? Here in the West I believe that most people (perhaps particularly those who are not "church-goers") when they hear the word "church", think either of the clergy or of the building – the parish church, as we might say. Yet in the Bible, out of all the chapters and verses where the word occurs, only *once* (and that is in the Old Testament) does it refer to a building.

The original word in Greek, and also in Latin, means "called" – or rather, "called out". The Church in which we are professing our belief is always people . . . people who are "called out" by God for a purpose: *His* purpose. And no one can even be a Christian at all, unless he or she is a member of that community which is called out from among all the people of Planet Earth to be in a true sense the people of God. And when God's people are mentioned in the Bible it is surprising how often the word HOLY is applied to them! "You are a holy people to the Lord." "You are a chosen race, a royal priesthood, a holy nation, God's own people."

Of course the Church is holy because it is God's creation, called out by Him to be a witness for Him to the world, to the very end of time. So we can express our belief in the Holy Catholic Church without claiming in any way that we, in our lives, are holy too! Yet, if we are to be *made* holy, it will only be by reason of belonging to that community and sharing in its life. You cannot be a Christian in isolation, you must be part of God's family. In fact the very earliest description of the Church says just that: "None of them said that anything he possessed was his own, they had all things in *common*". And you cannot be a Christian either unless you truly believe that your faith is a *catholic* faith, a *universal* faith, a faith that holds *true* in every country, in every century, in every kind of society to the end of the Age.

What a challenge! How can we possibly rise up to it? The answer is that we cannot do it alone. We can only face this challenge, the challenge to be part of God's Christian family, with the power of God's Spirit which first came to that small, frightened community at Pentecost, and then "they turned the world upside down".

21.
The Communion of Saints

This phrase in the Apostles' Creed is really an extension, a filling out, of the last: "I believe in the Holy Catholic Church". For, as we have seen, the Church is a community – or it is nothing. In fact it is much more than *a* community, it is God's creation, and its life is the life given by the Holy Spirit of God. Only in this sense can we believe that the Church is Holy. Yet because we can and do believe this we have to go on to express our belief in the holiness which each member of the community derives from being a member of the Holy Church, and that is exactly the meaning of the word "Saint" as it is used in this article of the Creed.

The saints – in every letter of St Paul and elsewhere in the New Testament – are simply the Christians, those small communities of men, women and children who, in one way or another, have been called to *be* the hands and feet and eyes and the life of the Master; to *be*, in Paul's word, "The Body of Christ".

So, in fact, the word "community" is itself not sufficient to express this truth. "Communion" is better, for it conveys with it the meaning of union *with* Christ, the Head of the Body, as well as of union with one another: "None of them said anything he possessed was his own – they had all things in common", above all their obedience to the risen, Living Lord.

Well, that's a very abstract, theological kind of statement. We may find it quite easy to say, but what does it mean in terms of our ordinary daily life? How do we carry it into this turbulent world so that it has a meaning, is recognizable, is capable of making an impact on society – however alienated from God that society may appear to be? There's a real paradox here. Because although it is absolutely necessary to understand the word "saint" in the way in which I have described it – one who is part of a community, a communion which is holy – the fact is that the word "saint" is today applied only to very special members of that Holy Communion, to those who, in their lives and deaths, have shown what sanctity, sainthood ought to mean.

I shall never forget one episode in the visit of Pope John Paul II to England a few years ago. It was that moment in Canterbury Cathedral when, at one point in the service, various members of the vast congregation, including the Pope and the Archbishop themselves, moved with a lighted candle and placed it in front of large photographs of some modern Christian martyrs: those who had been such witnesses (and that is the meaning of the word "martyr") to Christ as to have taken their place for ever in the ranks of God's saints. They were too many, alas, to tell of adequately here. But I found myself looking through the flickering candle flame into the eye of Archbishop Luwum of Uganda, of Martin Luther King of the United States, of Archbishop Romero of El Salvador, of Maximilian Kolbe of Poland, of Dietrich Bonhoeffer of Germany . . . and the candle flame created the halo of light around them. Each one in his own way and in his own country is representative of our world, of our violent, turbulent, passionate world. Each one bears witness to Truth against Falsehood, Light against Darkness, Love against Hatred. Each bears that witness by the giving up of his life. "No one takes my life from me", said Jesus. "I have power to lay it down and I have power to take it again"; and "unless a grain of wheat falls into the earth and dies, it remains alone, but if it dies it bears much fruit."

Yet the questions remain. How did they do it? and why? They were flesh and blood like us; ordinary sinful, weak people like us; living in a world which is our world.

They are the ones, the representative ones of that Communion of Saints which is Christ's Body to the end of the Age!

22.
The Forgiveness of Sins

There is a story of a boy returning from service on a Sunday who, when asked by his mother what subject the minister had chosen for his sermon replied, "Sin". "And what did he say about it?" "He was against it."

In the West today sermons are not very often preached about sin, and, if they are, it is quite usual for the preacher to avoid any definition of it if he can. That is not because ministers of the Church are less against it than they used to be, but because, in this immensely complex world, moral and ethical problems, the question of right and wrong, are difficult to disentangle. Murder is wrong: is abortion murder or something else? Idolatry is wrong: is economic security to the exclusion of every other national goal, a form of patriotism or of idolatry? And so on.

Part of the difficulty lies in using abstract terms — and "sin" is one of them — to define what is not abstract at all, but in fact something extremely and inescapably personal and subjective. I may be against "sin", but I know only too well the form and nature and consequence of my own sins. So that is why, in this article of the Creed, we say we believe in "the forgiveness" not of "sin", the abstract, but of "sins": my sins, your sins, society's sins, and the world's sins. As Christians, if we did not believe in their forgiveness, all the other articles of the Creed would be a useless list of stupendous truths which in the end could have no relevance to us at all.

Let me try to justify that statement. In the four Gospels we are not often presented with Jesus in a pulpit. Usually He is proclaiming the good news of the Kingdom of God out on the hillside to a great crowd; at the corner of a village street to a group of His followers; talking to this individual or that *where they are*. Often He uses simple stories or parables that a child can understand; often He uses His power to heal as that very "good news" He has come to bring.

But there is one sermon, the first He ever preached in His home synagogue at Nazareth, amongst His own family and friends – the people amongst whom He was brought up. For that sermon we have in St Luke's Gospel the text he preached from the words of the prophet Isaiah:

"The Spirit of the Lord is upon me, because he has anointed me to preach good news [the Gospel] to the poor . . . to proclaim release to the captive and recovery of sight to the blind, to set at liberty those who are oppressed, to proclaim the acceptable year of the Lord".

In that one text Jesus announces the meaning and purpose of His whole ministry, a kind of agenda for the years that lie ahead. And He says to that congregation, so that they will never be tempted to forget that sermon: "Today the Scripture has been fulfilled in your hearing." They were delighted at such "gracious words". Delighted, that is, until He went on to spell out their meaning. The meaning can be summed up in another phrase of His: "I have not come to call the righteous, but *sinners* to repentance".

As a result, we are told, the congregation "rose up and put Him out of the city" and tried to kill Him. This was because He claimed authority to forgive sins; because when He came to bring sight to the blind, hearing to the deaf, life to the dead, release to the captives, liberty to the oppressed, He was proclaiming the very heart of His message. And to those who heard Him it was a blasphemy, for they asked, "Who can forgive sins except God?" They stood mocking Him at the foot of Calvary for the same reason: "He saved others; Himself he can not save!"

I believe in the forgiveness of sins, my sins, because His claims are true and bring salvation . . . He is GOD.

23.
The Resurrection
of the Body

Have you noticed that the last few articles of the Creed, the ones that refer so directly to our own understanding of the Christian life, somehow refer back to those great mysteries which we have already proclaimed as our faith? The Church to which we belong is the direct creation, at Pentecost, of God's Holy Spirit. The forgiveness of sins is the direct result of the Passion and death of Christ, by which sin itself was conquered. And now, as we come to express our faith in the Resurrection of the Body, we know the full force of St Paul's words in his letter to the Christians of Corinth:

"If there is no resurrection of the dead, then Christ has not been raised . . . if Christ has not been raised your faith is futile . . . those who have fallen asleep in Christ have perished".

For all Christians the Resurrection itself, the Resurrection alone, is the truth by which we live. But is it just an historical event which took place on that first Easter morning nearly two thousand years ago? An event which assured Christ's followers, Peter and John and Mary Magdalene and the others, that He was indeed the conqueror of death? What about *us*? – here and alive in this world today but knowing one thing for certain, an absolutely sure fact which is inescapable and unavoidable: the fact that we shall die; the fact that this body of ours will one day return to dust.

Or will it? It is that question that we are answering when we say "I believe in the resurrection of the Body". And it was that same question which was argued about by the very first generation of Christians to whom St Paul was writing in Corinth.

A few years ago I had a holiday in Greece and went to visit that very place, Corinth, where so much of the ancient city still stands. It still is dominated by the ruins of the Roman Temple, still bears traces of the tribunal where Paul defended himself from the attacks of his adversaries before Proconsul Gallio who, we are told, "cared for none of these things".

But those first Christians cared greatly and questioned deeply about death, above all, about life after death. They cared not just about the Resurrection, but about the Resurrection of the Body. And Paul cared most of all: "How are the dead raised? With what kind of body do they come?" What a comfort to us to know that it is after all an enormously difficult question to answer, and that even Paul can only do so by showing that the really important issue, the really important question, is not "What is a body?", but "What is a body for?"

Dewi Morgan, who for many years was the Rector of a famous church in London, St Bride's, Fleet Street, wrote a splendid Easter sermon recently with the title "Being still 'me' in a heavenly body". Using a different and contemporary analogy, one which would appeal to the seekers of our day, he answered the question like this. "I am not as concerned about the reconstitution of my physical particles as I am about being able to do in the next life many of the things for which I used my body in this one . . . In the next life I do not want to be an anonymous, amorphous, uninteresting unit of spirituality lost in a great ocean of mystic being. I want to be ME."

"I want to be ME." If we accept this clause of the Apostles' Creed, however gropingly, fearfully and anxiously we may say it, that is the truth which – if our wish is granted – makes literally all the difference, all the difference between life and death. It is precisely *this* truth that St Paul is handing over to his little church in Corinth:

"What you sow is not the body which is to be, but a bare kernel, perhaps of wheat, or of some other grain, BUT GOD GIVES IT A BODY AS HE HAS CHOSEN."

24.
And the Life Everlasting

For the last assertion of our Christian faith as it is
expressed in the Apostles' Creed, we say: "I believe in
life everlasting." We don't say, "I hope there *may* be a
life after death." We certainly don't say, "I can prove
that there *is* a life after death." Nor are we so foolish as
to claim that the kind of life which will be ours after
death can be described in words. Even the great poet
Dante, writing as no one else has ever written about the
after-life, was not claiming to have *seen* Purgatory, or
Hell or Paradise with his own eyes. Any more than John
Bunyan claimed to follow his Pilgrim through the
heavenly gates: "The trumpets sounded for him on the
other side." A marvellously evocative phrase for the end
of the pilgrimage – but still "the other side".

So this affirmation is and must be exactly what the
writer of the letter to the Hebrews claimed for faith.
"Faith", he wrote, "is the *assurance* of things *hoped* for,
the conviction of things not seen . . ." And having gone

on to give examples of people who, like Abraham and Sarah and the patriarchs of old, had lived by faith, he sums it all up like this:

"These all died in faith not having received what was promised, but having seen it and greeted it *from afar* . . . Therefore God is not ashamed to be called their God, for He has prepared for them a city."

Of course in using language like this we immediately appear to open up a vast gulf, a chasm, between those who claim to hold an entirely scientific materialist view of the purpose of human existence and those who don't; a divide, if you like, between the religious and the secular – or whatever words you choose.

"Life everlasting", a life eternal, so fundamental a part of Christian belief, is "pie in the sky when you die", nothing more than a fairy story, to those who have no religious faith. Even to those who have, it is a constantly recurring challenge, and one which comes to those who have most sensibility, most compassion, most love – or at least, it is so in my experience. There is the challenge between our belief in the life everlasting and the fact of physical death. To see – as we can see on our television screens – a child dying of starvation and its mother watching death take that child out of her arms. To hear the bitter anguished poetry and music of Wilfred Owen's *War Requiem*:

What passing-bells for those who die as cattle?
Only the monstrous anger of the guns.

Only the stuttering rifles' rapid rattle
can patter out their hasty orisons.

To touch (as many of us have done and will do again)
the cold cheek of one deeply loved, by whose death-bed
we have been watching through the last hours and days
and nights of pain. Can it be true that they are already
moving into life? Everlasting life? Eternal life? (Whatever that may mean.)

This is the challenge for every single one of us, and
we must not try to evade it by saying the words of the
Creed and hoping for the best. Hoping against hope,
that is, that they are true.

For the Christian faith is the most life-affirming
religion there is. It begins in the first words of the Bible
with the magnificent affirmation "In the beginning God
created . . ." that is, gave Life where there was chaos.
And God said, "Let there be Light and there was Light
. . ." And the Christian faith goes on to declare that
God Himself has shared in the life of His creation. "I
am", says Christ, "the way, the truth and the Life", and
to declare also that each single person receives that life,
"our life is united with Christ in God".

So, as we say those last words of the Creed we are
simply stating everything as what we already KNOW!

25.
Amen

We have come to the end of the great affirmations of the
Apostles' Creed. All that is left for us to say is that small
Hebrew word which for centuries has been used by Jew
and Christian alike to express a great longing that their
prayers may be heard. And yet I dare to say that most of
us who use it are so familiar with it that it is nothing
more than the full-stop at the end of a sentence:
AMEN!

AMEN! It is a Hebrew word, yet it crosses all the
boundaries of language and culture and nation, and it
spans not only centuries but millennia. As others have
said, "Small is beautiful."

We have learnt to recognize it. And what more
beautiful an acknowledgement of this could there be
than the word which, in its Hebrew origin, means True
and Faithful and Certain, the word which, at the end of
a prayer or a proclamation, means "So shall it be! So be
it!" When we use it at the end of reciting the Creed we

aren't just committing ourselves as individuals to the acceptance of the truths the Creed expresses — although of course we are indeed doing that. But we are doing something which from the earliest days of the Christian Church has been done to proclaim our oneness, our unity in faith. It is claimed by scholars that, at the beginning, the only creed required of one who wished to be baptized and taken into the community, was "JESUS IS LORD". St Paul, writing from prison and allowing himself to glory in the growth of that little church at Ephesus, told them, "There is one body and one spirit — one Lord, one faith, one baptism, one God and Father of us all." And the Creed that we recite today in every corner of the world is for the safeguarding of that Oneness till the end of time. The trouble, as with so much else in the Christian Church today, is that we like to use the Creed not as an expression of faith, but as an escape from the need to think and to act and to live by that faith.

"What do you Christians believe?" says Everyman. "You can find it in the Creed", we reply, using it as a kind of map. Not perhaps an ordnance survey map, which sets out every country lane and footpath and stream, but at least a map which features the towns and cities and the main motorways between them. Of course, the Creed is like that, it does help us to find our way through all the complexities and theological conflicts which have appeared through the centuries since Pentecost. But many Christians today would really prefer to do without maps altogether, claiming that the

Creed has created more disunity than unity; that it does not provide clear answers to the problems of our turbulent world. Such Christians would greatly prefer an "automatic pilot" which brings the plane to a safe landing without any human intervention at all.

That is quite an understandable wish, until you remember that the faith enshrined in the Creed is something which infinitely transcends and outshines the words in which it is written, words which are all we have to express the inexpressible, words which can never do more than help us to find our way home and to keep us together when we are tempted to wander away. Three hundred years ago that old fisherman, Izaak Walton, wrote some wise words about the difficulty of faith and the problems thrown up by the words of the Creed: "Almighty God intends not to lead us to Heaven by hard questions, but by meekness and charity."

And we turn again to that great English poet, William Blake who said this:

> I give you the end of a golden string
> Only wind it into a ball.
> It will bring you in at Heaven's gate
> Built in Jerusalem's wall.

AMEN!   AMEN!

Also available in Fount Paperbacks

Naught for your Comfort
TREVOR HUDDLESTON

'To recommend a book by such a fascinating and controversial man would be superfluous; to ban it, as the South African censors will certainly do, ineffective. It will be widely read here and – more important – there.'

Colin Welch, Daily Telegraph

Let My People Go
ALBERT LUTHULI

'Luthuli's love for his country transcends his loyalty to any one racial group within it. This book will surely convince the world that the Nobel Prize was most justly awarded to its author.'

Trevor Huddleston, Sunday Times

Instrument of thy Peace
ALAN PATON

'Worthy of a permanent place on the short shelf of enduring classics of the life of the Spirit.'

Henry P. Van Dusen,
Union Theological Seminary

Miracle on the River Kwai
ERNEST GORDON

'This description of the reality of Christian love, discovered in the hell of unspeakable prisoner-of-war conditions, says more to the average man than the most brilliant treatise of apologetics.'

David H. D. Read

Also available in Fount Paperbacks

The Mind of St Paul
WILLIAM BARCLAY

'There is a deceptive simplicity about this fine exposition of Pauline thought at once popular and deeply theological. The Hebrew and Greek backgrounds are described and all the main themes are lightly but fully treated.'   *The Yorkshire Post*

The Plain Man Looks at the Beatitudes
WILLIAM BARCLAY

'. . . the author's easy style should render it . . . valuable and acceptable to the ordinary reader.'   *Church Times*

The Plain Man Looks at the Lord's Prayer
WILLIAM BARCLAY

Professor Barclay shows how this prayer that Jesus gave to his disciples is at once a summary of Christian teaching and a pattern for all prayers.

The Plain Man's Guide to Ethics
WILLIAM BARCLAY

The author demonstrates beyond all possible doubt that the Ten Commandments are the most relevant document in the world today and are totally related to mankind's capacity to live and make sense of it all within a Christian context.

Ethics in a Permissive Society
WILLIAM BARCLAY

How do we as Christians deal with such problems as drug taking, the 'pill', alcohol, morality of all kinds, in a society whose members are often ignorant of the Church's teaching? Professor Barclay approaches a difficult and vexed question with his usual humanity and clarity, asking what Christ himself would say or do in our world today.

Also available in Fount Paperbacks

BOOKS BY WILLIAM BARCLAY

Jesus of Nazareth

'The book is in Dr Barclay's usual readable and straightforward style and is quite worthy of the film, as the film was of the book.'
Life and Work

In the Hands of God
Ed. BY RITA SNOWDEN

William Barclay's *British Weekly* articles have brought comfort, understanding and pleasure to thousands. These articles help us to take a fresh look at our own lives and the people in them.

Prayers for Young People

Morning and evening prayers for every week of the year, designed to help young people to pray, and with a fine introductory chapter on 'You and Your Prayers'.

More Prayers for Young People

'William Barclay has provided excellent help . . . All Dr Barclay's well-known virtues of clarity and soundness are present.'
Church Times

The Plain Man Looks at the Apostles' Creed

'An excellent book for a serious-minded Church study group . . . It would also provide . . . the right material for a series of talks on the Apostles' Creed. Once again Professor Barclay has done a great service for his fellow Christians in the Church.'
Expository Times

Also available in Fount Paperbacks

BOOKS BY C. S. LEWIS

The Abolition of Man

'It is the most perfectly reasoned defence of Natural Law (Morality) I have ever seen, or believe to exist.'

Walter Hooper

Mere Christianity

'He has a quite unique power for making theology an attractive, exciting and fascinating quest.'

Times Literary Supplement

God in the Dock

'This little book . . . consists of some brilliant pieces . . . This is just the kind of book to place into the hands of an intellectual doubter . . . It has been an unalloyed pleasure to read.'

Marcus Beverley, Christian Herald

The Great Divorce

'Mr Lewis has a rare talent for expressing spiritual truth in fresh and striking imagery and with uncanny acumen . . . it contains many flashes of deep insight and exposures of popular fallacies.'

Church Times

Fount Paperbacks

Fount is one of the leading paperback publishers of religious books and below are some of its recent titles.

- [ ] THE WAY OF ST FRANCIS Murray Bodo £2.50
- [ ] GATEWAY TO HOPE Maria Boulding £1.95
- [ ] LET PEACE DISTURB YOU Michael Buckley £1.95
- [ ] DEAR GOD, MOST OF THE TIME YOU'RE QUITE NICE Maggie Durran £1.95
- [ ] CHRISTIAN ENGLAND VOL 3 David L Edwards £4.95
- [ ] A DAZZLING DARKNESS Patrick Grant £3.95
- [ ] PRAYER AND THE PURSUIT OF HAPPINESS Richard Harries £1.95
- [ ] THE WAY OF THE CROSS Richard Holloway £1.95
- [ ] THE WOUNDED STAG William Johnston £2.50
- [ ] YES, LORD I BELIEVE Edmund Jones £1.75
- [ ] THE WORDS OF MARTIN LUTHER KING Coretta Scott King (Ed) £1.75
- [ ] BOXEN C S Lewis £4.95
- [ ] THE CASE AGAINST GOD Gerald Priestland £2.75
- [ ] A MARTYR FOR THE TRUTH Grazyna Sikorska £1.95
- [ ] PRAYERS IN LARGE PRINT Rita Snowden £2.50
- [ ] AN IMPOSSIBLE GOD Frank Topping £1.95
- [ ] WATER INTO WINE Stephen Verney £2.50

All Fount paperbacks are available at your bookshop or newsagent, or they can be ordered by post from Fount Paperbacks, Cash Sales Department, G.P.O. Box 29, Douglas, Isle of Man, British Isles. Please send purchase price, plus 15p per book, maximum postage £3. Customers outside the U.K. send purchase price, plus 15p per book. Cheque, postal or money order. No currency.

NAME (Block letters) _____

ADDRESS _____

_____